Secrets of Summer

Logan Smith

BookLeaf Publishing

India | USA | UK

Presentation by *BookLeaf Publishing*

Web: www.bookleafpub.com

E-mail: info@bookleafpub.com

ISBN: 9789363312210

First edition 2024

*To my amazing mom. The first person to tell me
I could be anything I wanted.*

Want

When we get what we want, we sometimes
realize that wanting that thing to begin with was
a mistake. A mistake we must now live with.

Love

In life some love many, some love few, and some never love. I've been lucky to not be the last.

Secrets

Secrets eat away inside. Secrets soon revealed.
Some know, some don't. All must learn the truth
so the torture can stop.

Thunderstorms

Lightning streaks across the black sky, lighting up the world for a few seconds. The sharp crackle of thunder moments later. Finally the peaceful sound of a downpour of rain. This is nature's beauty, the first thunderstorm of summer.

Day

What does day mean to you? To some it means daylight, to others it means work. To me it means an opportunity to have fun and make the most of life with friends and family. It means warmth, life, and joy.

Pool

Swimming in the pool. Light as air, the feeling of flying. The peace of drifting and floating. The cool, calming water surrounding us. The pool is one of the true joys of summer.

Beach

Sand underfoot, waves crashing a few feet away, and seagulls screeching overhead. The beach is a must during summer. The ocean washes away sadness and pain, replacing those dark emotions with laughter and delight.

Friends

Summer is a time best spent with friends. Movie nights, beach days, time spent in the pool, getting ice cream, going to out to dinners, and listening to our favorite musicians. These are but a few ways my friends and I choose to spend our summers.

Family

Family is everything. Family isn't always about blood. You get to choose your family. Family is a huge part of life. Everyone has some form of family, even if it's close friends that have become your chosen family. My family chose me when I was a newborn and I'm grateful for that every day.

Vacation

Summer vacation. Traveling to interesting cities, and visiting family in far away towns. Nashville, Orlando, Boston, Colorado Springs, and Lake George. Some of the wonderful places I've been lucky enough to visit on vacation.

Birthday

Her birthday is finally here. The midpoint of summer is now meant to celebrate. We didn't know her two years ago and now none of us can imagine life without her. We met her two years ago in a little tiny room. She is the heart of our family. niece to my sister and I, granddaughter to my mom and dad, daughter to my brother and his wife. Her name, Isabel.

Darkness

Darkness isn't always bad. Darkness provides cooler weather and peace during summer. It also provides an opportunity for fireflies to shine. Without darkness the beauty of the night sky and nature's bioluminescence would not be visible. Darkness is full of wonder if you know what to look for.

Fireworks

Showers of sparks and bright, shining bursts of light. Alluring explosions midair. Fireworks used to celebrate during Fourth of July. A summer favorite.

Bonfire

Cracking flames, sparks flying. The smell of sweet smokiness. Summer bonfires are amazing. Toasting marshmallows, drying off from swimming all day. The perfect end to a day.

Stars

The stars twinkle in the night sky. The sky so clear in the warmer weather. Diamonds in the heavens, not meant for us to touch or spend.

Ice Cream

Sweet and creamy, cold and frosty. Delicious ice cream. This a staple of summer. So many flavors including chocolate, vanilla, and strawberry. Ice cream is one of the best parts of summer.

Concerts

Wading through crowds of people. Listening to roaring music. Fighting our way to get as close to the stage as possible. We get to see our favorite artists perform live. We love going to concerts.

Vinyl

Flipping through the dusty boxes searching for gold. No not the precious metal, but vinyl records. They hold wonderful secrets within. The sweet music comes singing from the record player, day and night.

Breeze

Windows open, a warm, soft breeze blows into the room. On it the wonderful scents of summer are carried. The breeze brings memories flooding back of summers past. Good and bad, painful and joyous.

Florida

Florida is known for citrus and sunshine. To me
it is so much more. It's family, love, and fun.
Many fun secrets and wonderful restaurants.
Florida a second home.

Magic

The world around us is full of magic. Nature, family, love, friends, and everything else wonderful in life, are all forms of magic.

www.ingramcontent.com/pod-product-compliance
Lightning Source LLC
LaVergne TN
LVHW041302200726